ESL
OPERATIONS
TECHNIQUES FOR LEARNING WHILE DOING

Gayle Nelson   **Thomas Winters**

Newbury House Publishers, Inc. / Rowley / Massachusetts / 01969

Library of Congress Cataloging in Publication Data

Nelson, Gayle L   1947-
    ESL operations.

    Includes indexes.
    SUMMARY: Presents a variety of "operations," or
procedures for doing something using a natural sequence
of events, for use in teaching English as a second
language by involving students in practical, active use of language.
    1. English language—Text-books for foreigners.
[1. English language—Textbooks for foreigners]
I. Winters, Thomas A., 1945-   joint author.
II. Whistler, T. D.   III. Title.
PE1128.N35   428.2'4   79-26911
ISBN 0-88377-149-7

Illustrations by **T. D. Whistler**

NEWBURY HOUSE PUBLISHERS, INC.

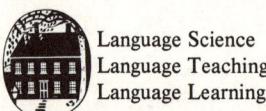
Language Science
Language Teaching
Language Learning

ROWLEY, MASSACHUSETTS 01969

Copyright © 1980 by Newbury House Publishers, Inc. All rights reserved. No part of this book may be reproduced or transmitted in any form or by any means, electronic or mechanical, including photocopying, recording, or by any information storage and retrieval system, without permission in writing from the Publisher.

First printing: February 1980
5   4   3

Printed in the U.S.A.

Foreword

The term "operation," as used for the type of procedures found in this book, has found almost universal acceptance. It is used by teachers in a wide range of situations, from the School for International Training in Brattleboro, Vermont, to the Saudi Arabian Defense School in Jeddah, Saudi Arabia. It is unclear who first used the word operation in this sense, but the influences are many, as are the number of teaching methodologies with which it is compatible. Operations have been and can be used with audio-lingual materials, notional/functional/communicative materials, situational reinforcement, total physical response, and the Silent Way, among others.

Acknowledgments

We wish to express our thanks to the students and staff of the School for International Training for their suggestions and support, especially Phillip Stantial, Elizabeth Tannenbaum, and Jan Gallegher for their time and effort in getting this project off the ground. A special debt of gratitude is expressed to our linguist, Mary Clark, for helping us with the grammar components in each operation, and to Ray Clark for his continuous guidance.

Particular thanks are due Eleanor Boone, Tom Schmid, Ralph Nelson, and Dora Nelson for their original ideas and their helpful comments.

Contents

Foreword	iii
Acknowledgments	iv
What Is an Operation?	1
Why Use Operations?	1
When to Use Operations	2
How to Use Operations	3
How to Use This Book	8
Classroom Activities	**11**
Drawing a Picture	12
Coloring the Picture	13
Playing with Numbers	14
Writing On and Erasing a Blackboard	15
Using a Table of Contents	16
Using an Index	17
Using a Dictionary	18
Operating a Cassette Recorder	19
Making a Paper Hat	20
Making a Paper Airplane	22
Sharpening a Pencil	24
Household Activities	**27**
Lighting a Candle	28
Setting a Table	29
Setting an Alarm Clock	30
Threading a Needle	32
Sewing on a Button	34
Pounding a Nail	36
Potting a Plant	38
Games and Exercises	**39**
Touching Your Toes	41
Hopping on One Leg	42
Blowing Up a Balloon	43
Playing Jacks	44

Contents

Games and Exercises (continued)

Relaxation Breathing	46
Playing Dice	47
Playing Concentration with Cards	48
Playing War	50

Food and Recipes   53

Eating Cookies	55
Eating an Apple	56
Making a Cup of Coffee	57
Making Instant Pudding	58
Making a Peanut Butter and Jelly Sandwich	60

Communication   63

Mailing a Letter	64
Using a Pay Telephone	66
Sending a Telegram	68
Wiring Money	70

Miscellany   73

Writing a Check	74
Opening a Pull-Top Can	76
Using a Vending Machine	78
Finding an Apartment	80
Using a Map	82
Filling in a Form	84
Key Verb Index	87
Grammar Notes Index	89

What Is an Operation?

An operation is a procedure for doing something, using a natural sequence of events. It may involve manipulating a piece of equipment, such as operating a tape recorder; or it may relate to skill development, such as using an index or a dictionary; or it may involve body movement, such as touching your toes. The procedure can be as simple as making a cup of coffee or as complex as filling in a form.

The use of language is the essential factor leading the student through the process of correctly completing the operation. In other words, Student A gives directions to Student B, and unless those directions are correct, Student B will not successfully complete the operation. For example, in the operation on Mailing a Letter, Student A must instruct Student B to fold the letter before Student B can put the letter in the envelope. Language, therefore, is the medium that enables the student to complete the process, and the process is a vehicle for learning the language. The meaning of the language is made clear by the action and the action reinforces the language. There is, therefore, tactile and visual memory as well as linguistic memory.

An operation is usually a set of instructions delivered in the form of commands. The most useful format is called the 8×8, a series of eight commands, each command not exceeding eight words. Students are better able to remember and work with sentences of eight words or less. If an operation is much longer, they have more difficulty remembering the steps. In some more complex operations, lines do exceed the eight-word limit. These operations would be used in a more advanced English class, however, where students would be able to handle the more elaborate structures.

Why Use Operations?

Operations are an effective way for students to use the language actively in a purposeful, functional manner. Since students are physically responding to the words, the language has concrete meaning. As Student A reads the operation to Student B, Student B must focus on the message because he is forced to show whether he has understood. He demonstrates his understanding by doing the action.

Operations can be used for teaching and practicing verb tenses. The verbs used in operations are characteristically high-frequency action verbs, such as put, hold, open, close, take, give, and let; and two-word verbs, such as turn on, pick up, fill in, and stand up. Depending on the level of the class, the teacher may vary the verb phrase by using different verb tenses. For example, if the class were working on the past tense, the question "What did you do?" might be asked at the completion of the operation, thus causing the student to change the verbs to the past form.

Operations can be designed around students' specific needs, for example, Using a Dictionary, an Index, a Map, or a Pay Telephone, thereby increasing their motivation and retention. They can also be used for cross-cultural situations, such as Finding an Apartment or Writing a Check, to facilitate a student's entry into the American culture.

Operations add variety to the class, and students enjoy doing them. The teacher withdraws from direct participation early in the lesson; therefore, *the students are able to perform and practice by themselves.* Because operations are short, they can easily be covered in a class period.

When to Use Operations

Operations should be used as a supplement to the regular curriculum. For example, after working with irregular past forms, the teacher may select an operation, such as Lighting a Candle, that uses several irregular verbs. After the student has completed the operation, the teacher asks, "What did you do?" eliciting the response, "I lit the match and then held the flame next to the candle wick."

Operations can be used at any level of English competency, although they work best at beginning and intermediate levels. An operation that is appropriate for the level of the class should be selected. The operation on Eating a Cookie works well in a beginning class because the students have an opportunity to use verbs that they know, such as open, close, take, and give. For beginning classes, the operations are purposely short. Advanced classes may also use operations; for example, the operation on Filling in a Form may be used in a class that is preparing for university study in the United States.

Operations can be used as supplementary activities when working on verb tenses, intonation and stress patterns, vocabulary building, cultural information, word order, possessive pronouns, locative phrases (prepositional phrases of place), questions, or adverbs. They are recyclable in that the teacher may use a specific operation once and then return it a few weeks later, changing the point of emphasis. For example, the focus may be a specific verb tense in the initial presentation and the intonation patterns in the second presentation.

How to Use Operations

Operations can be used in a variety of ways and as a supplement to a variety of methods. Three possible presentations are given here, the second two being variations of the first. Each class and teacher should, however, develop its own way of using operations. These examples are suggestions to help a class that is beginning to use operations; they are not set criteria.

Example 1   The teacher is responsible for setting up the environment and bringing in necessary materials. The teacher should have the operation memorized. In the initial presentation, teachers introduce the piece of equipment or materials to be used, pointing out the parts and introducing unfamiliar vocabulary. They then model the sequence of actions, demonstrating the use of a piece of equipment, making something, or doing some action. For example, in the operation on Mailing a Letter, the teacher says, "Fold the letter to fit the envelope" and then completes the action by folding the letter to fit the envelope. The teacher says each line of the operation and then performs the action until the operation is completed. The students then open their textbooks. The teacher may lead the class through a choral repetition, listening for stress patterns, pronunciation, and intonation.

Two students now perform the operation. For example:

Student A: Fold the letter to fit the envelope.
Student B: (folds the letter to fit the envelope)
Student A: Put the letter in the envelope.
Student B: (puts the letter in the envelope)

The student giving directions has his book open, and the student receiving directions has his book closed. If the class were working on a particular verb tense or grammar point, a question-response sequence might be used after the completion of each step to provide practice in that particular tense or grammar point. For example, if the class were studying locative phrases (prepositional phrases of location), the question-response sequence might go as follows:

Student A: Put the plate in the center of the placemat.
Student B: (puts the plate in the center of the placemat)
Student A: Where is the plate?
Student B: The plate is in the center of the placemat.
Student A: Put the napkin to the left of the plate.
Student B: (puts the napkin to the left of the plate)
Student A: Where did you put the napkin?
Student A: I put the napkin to the left of the plate.

In summary, the first presentation is as follows:
A. Introduction
   1. The teacher introduces the materials and new vocabulary.
   2. The teacher gives the directions and performs the sequence of actions.
   3. The students open their textbooks.
   4. The teacher may choose to lead the class through a choral repetition.
   5. Two students perform the complete operation. After completing the operation once, the students switch roles and perform the operation again. The class observes the two students.
B. Class practice
   1. The class divides into pairs and performs the operation, each student taking a turn at giving and receiving directions. The student giving directions has his book open and reads the operation. The student receiving directions has his book closed and performs the actions.
   2. The students again perform the operation, but with their books closed. They may vary the words, as long as the meaning is retained and the sentences are grammatically correct.

Example 2   The students read the operation silently to themselves. After they finish, the teacher asks if they have any questions regarding pronunciation, vocabulary, grammar, or overall comprehension. After the questions have been answered, two students or the teacher and a student perform the operation, one giving directions and the other responding. If a class is familiar with operations, this modeling stage may not be necessary. The class then divides into pairs and performs the operation. For example:

   Student A: Take a book.
   Student B: (takes a book)
   Student A: Open it to the first page.
   Student B: (opens it to the first page)

The student giving directions has his book open, and the student receiving directions has his book shut. After the operation is completed, the students change roles and do it again.

   The class then divides into pairs to perform the operation. Each student first gives and then follows directions. After everyone has completed both roles in the operation, the students close their books and again perform the operation as well as they are able. The students may vary the words, as long as the meaning is retained and the sentences are grammatically correct.

In summary, the second presentation is as follows:
A. Introduction
   1. Students read the operation.
   2. Students ask questions regarding vocabulary, pronunciation, grammar, meaning, etc.
   3. Two students or the teacher and a student may perform the operation, one giving directions and the other following the directions. After completing the operation once, they switch roles and perform it again. The class observes.
B. Class practice
   1. The class divides into pairs and performs the operation, each student taking a turn at giving and following directions. The student giving directions has his book open and reads the operation. The student receiving directions has his book closed and performs the actions.
   2. The students again perform the operation, but with books closed. They may vary the words, as long as the meaning is retained and the sentences are grammatically correct.

Example 3 Really a variation of the first two types, this presentation can be used after students are familiar with the pair procedure. The advantage of this variation is that the task of figuring out the operation is given to the students. The teacher acts as a resource person who answers specific individual questions. In this variation, the class divides into pairs and the teacher assigns the operation. The teacher should select an operation that the students will be able to do on their own. The teacher is also responsible for each pair having the necessary materials. The students then perform the operation. Student A begins with his book open and reads the operation to Student B. Student B has his book closed and follows the directions. When Student B has finished the last step of the operation, they switch roles. Student A closes his book and Student B opens his book and reads the operation to Student A. After both students have performed both roles, they both close their books. Again, Student A gives directions to Student B. He may vary the words as long as the meaning is retained and the sentences are grammatically correct. When finished, Student B gives directions to Student A.

In summary, this third variation is as follows:
A. First performance
   1. Student A has his book open and reads the operation to Student B.
   2. Student B has his book closed and follows Student A's directions.

B. Second performance
   1. Student B has his book open and reads the operation to Student A.
   2. Student A has his book closed and follows Student B's directions.
C. Third and fourth performance
   1. Both students close their books. Student A gives the directions. He may vary the words as long as the meaning is retained and the sentences are grammatically correct. Student B follows the directions and performs the operation.
   2. Student B gives the directions and Student A follows them.

To further clarify the pair interaction between students, here is an example.

Using an Index: An Example of Pair Interaction   Student A has his book open. Student B has his book closed. Student A reads the operation from the book, one step at a time, and Student B responds.

   Student A: Take a book.
   Student B: (takes a book)
   Student A: Open it to the first page.
   Student B: (opens it to the first page)
   Student A: Find the index page or pages.
   Student B: (finds the index page or pages)
   Student A: Look for the word or topic that you want.
   Student B: (looks for the word or topic that he/she wants)
   Student A: See what page it's on.
   Student B: (sees what page it's on)
   Student A: Turn to that page.
   Student B: (turns to that page)

After Student B has finished, Student A asks, "What did you do?" and Student B tells what he did in his own words. For example:

   I picked up the book on operations and opened it. I found the index in the last few pages and then I looked for the operation on Using an Index. I found that operation and the page it was on. Then I turned to that page and found the correct operation.

Now Student B opens his book and gives directions to Student A. Student A closes his book and follows the directions.

After both students have completed the operation, the teacher asks them to write a paragraph titled "How to Use an Index." In the paragraph, they are to use transition words, such as first, second, next, then, afterward, and finally.

The effectiveness of an operation lies in the interaction between the students working in pairs—the speaking, the listening, the understanding, and the doing.

Ideas for presenting and using operations are many. Students can try some of these:

1. Prepare operation presentations and present them to the class.
2. Write their own operations, bring in necessary materials, and perform them in class.
3. Write each step of an operation on an index card, mix up the steps, and then give them to another student, who puts them in the correct order and performs the operation.
4. Illustrate each step of an operation on separate index cards, and then give them to another student, who puts them in the correct order and writes an operation or paragraph to match the illustrations.
5. Mime an original operation while other students watch, guess the activity, and then explain it orally.

In order to give students additional practice in spoken English, add appropriate words or phrases to the commands, thus providing transitions or creating polite requests. For example, the operation Using a Table of Contents can be modified in the following manner:

Please take a book.
Now open it to the first page.
Next find the table of contents.
Look down the left-hand margin, *please.*
Now pick out the chapter or topic that you want.
Next you follow a line across to the right-hand margin.
Please see what page the chapter begins on.
Finally, you're ready to turn to that page.

Other ways of introducing commands include:

Would (Will) you please . . .
At this point, you should . . .
Now try to . . .
Next you can . . .
You will (can, may should) now . . .
Would you mind _____ ing . . .

Operations also provide excellent practice in asking questions. If the class is learning or practicing a specific verb tense, the following chart provides examples of the kinds of questions that may be used:

Verb Tense	Sample Questions
Present continuous	What are you doing?
Past	What did you do?
Future	What will you do? What are you going to do?
Present perfect	What have you just done?
Past continuous	What were you doing a minute ago?
Future continuous	What will you be doing next?

Students can write and/or ask other questions, including yes-no questions and wh- questions. Some questions are:

Who lit the match?
Did he put coffee into her cup?
How are you pouring the water?
Where does the fork go?
Should I write down the telephone number?
Why do you write checks?
What should I do with the needle?

Students can write and/or ask questions before, during, or after an operation.

How to Use This Book

The operations in this book are divided into six categories. Within each category, the operations are sequenced in order of difficulty, so that the later operations require a higher level of vocabulary and a greater knowledge of grammatical structures than do the earlier ones. Operations were selected on the basis of their accessibility and adaptability. Therefore, most of the operations in this book make use of simple materials or materials that are easily obtainable and can be used in the classroom. A few of the operations use materials that are often inaccessible, but these operations can be mimed, for example, Using a Vending Machine and Opening a Pull-Top Can.

The format is the same for each operation. The title is given first, followed by the materials needed to perform the operation. Key words that occur in the operation are listed, with the verbs to the right of the other words. Next comes the operation itself, broken down into steps. After the operation, grammar notes are presented, including structures that occur repeatedly in the operation or that are likely to cause students particular difficulty. The grammar notes are mainly for the use of teachers. The final section gives follow-up activities that relate to the operation. Students should have performed the operation at least once before they do the follow-up activities. The follow-up section includes activities that are more creative, such as writing an original operation or a story. Questions that are given can be assigned as homework or done in class. The section also gives ideas for discussion, connected discourse, and games.

Commonly accepted terms are used when referring to grammar points. The one term that may need further clarification is "locative phrase." A locative phrase is a prepositional phrase of location or place. For example, in the sentence, "Put the plate on the table," the phrase "on the table" is a locative phrase. It answers the question "Where?"

Use this book as a guide. One does not need to use all the operations or necessarily to use them in the given sequence. These operations should be adapted to meet the specific needs of an individual classroom.

CLASSROOM ACTIVITIES

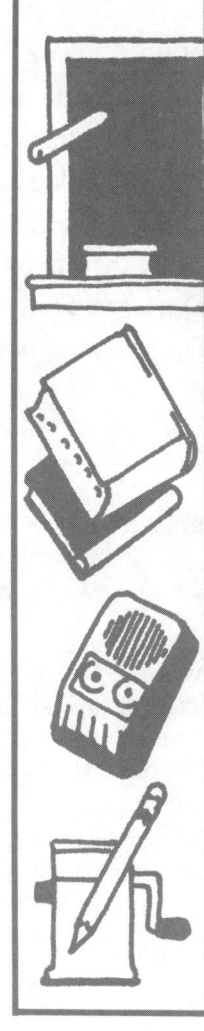

Drawing a Picture

Materials paper, pencils

Key words
next to   over   draw
in   around
between   near

Operation
1. Draw a lake.
2. Draw two trees next to the lake.
3. Draw a rock between the trees.
4. Draw a fish in the lake.
5. Draw the sun over the lake.
6. Draw two birds near the trees.
7. Draw grass around the lake.

Grammar notes   locative phrases
count and noncount nouns
definite and indefinite articles

Follow up
1. Dictate the operation. Student A reads the operation to Student B. Student B writes down what Student A says. After you're finished, check your work with your text. Change roles, so Student A becomes Student B, and do it again.
2. Write an operation on drawing a human body, an article of clothing, or a Halloween pumpkin.

Coloring the Picture

Materials   the picture from the operation Drawing a Picture, colors, pencils

Key words
frog   color   do

Operation
1. Color the lake blue.
2. Color the trees green and brown.
3. Draw a frog on the rock.
4. Color the frog green.
5. Do not color the fish.
6. Color the sun yellow.
7. Do not color the birds.
8. Color the grass green.

Grammar notes   shift from "a" to "the"
formation of negatives

Follow up
1. Do the operation again and substitute other adjectives in the pattern. For example: Color the frog red. Color the sun purple.
2. Experiment with your vocabulary. Write an operation for drawing and coloring a picture. Then read your operation to another student, and he will follow your directions. Continue until the picture is finished. Change roles.

Playing with Numbers

Materials   paper, pencils

Key words
in your head
sum

remember
subtract
multiply

divide
add

Operation

1. In your head, add 5 and 7 and 3.
2. Remember the sum.
3. Subtract 5 from the sum.
4. Multiply by 7.
5. Divide by 2.
6. Add 5 to the total.
7. Write down the number.

Grammar notes   verbs that take particular prepositions

Follow up
1. After each step, Student A asks a yes/no question. For example, "Did you add 5, 7, and 3?" Student B answers the question.
2. Student A gives Student B a more complicated mathematical problem. For example, Student A says, "Add 116 and 279. Now subtract 189 from the total." Continue giving directions until the problem is completed. Change roles.
3. Write an operation on averaging numbers.

Writing On and Erasing a Blackboard

Materials   a blackboard, chalk, an eraser

Key words
blackboard	eraser	pick up
chalk	near	hold
tray		erase

Operation
1. Pick up a piece of chalk.
2. Hold it near the blackboard.
3. Write your name on the blackboard.
4. Stop writing.
5. Put the chalk in the chalk tray.
6. Pick up the eraser.
7. Hold it near the blackboard.
8. Erase the blackboard.

Grammar notes   locative phrases
compound nouns

Follow up
1. Do it again and creatively use the language. Student A gives directions to Student B for drawing a picture or writing on the blackboard. For example:

   Student A: Draw a clown.
   Student B: (draws a clown)
   Student A: Draw a duck on top of the clown's head.

   Continue until the picture is completed. Then change roles.
2. Rewrite the operation adding descriptive adjectives to each step.

Using a Table of Contents

Materials   a book with a table of contents

Key words
table of contents	topic	pick out
left-hand	line	follow
margin	across	turn to
chapter	right-hand	

Operation
1. Take a book.
2. Open it to the first page.
3. Find the table of contents.
4. Look down the left-hand margin.
5. Pick out the chapter or topic that you want.
6. Follow a line across to the right-hand margin.
7. See what page the chapter begins on.
8. Turn to that page.

Grammar notes   locative phrases
two-word verbs
"that" clause

Follow up
1. Do the operation again and add transition words and phrases. For example, "*First,* take a book. *Now* open it to the first page. *OK, next you* find the table of contents. . . ."
2. Discuss the various divisions in a book (forewords, appendixes, introductions, indexes, chapters, etc.).
3. Make a book with pictures or assignments that you've written and make a table of contents for the book. Be sure to number the pages, choose chapter titles, etc.

Using an Index

Materials   a book with an index

Key words
last	page	find
few	topic	look for
		see

Operation

1. Take a book.
2. Open it to the last few pages.
3. Find the index page or pages.
4. Look for the word or topic that you want.
5. See what page it's on.
6. Turn to that page.

Grammar notes   "that" clause
indirect question

Follow up
1. Do the operation again and use modal auxiliaries to make polite requests. For example, "*Would* you *please* take a book? Now you *may* open it to the last few pages. . . ."
2. Close your books. Student A completes the operation without interruption. He tells what he is doing while he is doing it. For example, "I'm taking a book and opening it to the last few pages."
3. Rewrite the operation as a paragraph. Use transition words, such as first, second, next, then, afterward, and finally.

Using a Dictionary

Materials   a dictionary, a word to be looked up

Key words

first	dictionary	look at
second	section	fall
letter	top	
	definition	

Operation

1. Look at the first letter of the word.
2. Open the dictionary.
3. Find the section with words starting with that letter.
4. Look at the second letter of the word.
5. Find the words starting with those two letters.
6. Look at the words at the top of the page in the dictionary.
7. Notice if your word falls between them.
8. Find the word and read the definition.

Grammar notes   -ing phrases used as noun modifiers
ordinal expressions
"if" clause

Follow up
1. Do the operation again and add phrases that make the steps polite. For example, "*Please* look at the first letter of the word. *Now would you please* open the dictionary...."
2. List and describe the various sections of the dictionary.
3. Rewrite the operation as a paragraph. Use the past tense, and combine some of the sentences.

Operating a Cassette Recorder

Materials   a cassette recorder, a cassette

Key words

recorder	forward	plug in	rewind
button	tape	eject	play
cassette		insert	record
cover		advance	release

Operation

1. Plug in the recorder (or check the batteries).
2. Push the Stop/Eject button to open the recorder.
3. Insert a cassette and close the cover.
4. Push the Fast Forward button to advance the tape.
5. Push the Rewind button to rewind the tape.
6. Push the Play button to listen.
7. Push the Play and Record buttons to record.
8. Push the Stop/Eject button to eject or release the tape.

Grammar notes   infinitive clauses of purpose
verbs used as adjectives

Follow up
1. Use the recorder to interview each other, do news broadcasts, read stories, do a soap opera, or sing songs.
2. Tape a classroom conversation, transcribe it, and correct any grammar mistakes.

Making a Paper Hat

Materials   paper

Key words

in half	bottom	fold
folded	rectangular	unfold
center		bring

Operation

1. Fold the paper in half with the folded edge up.
2. Fold the paper from left to right.
3. Unfold the paper, leaving a line down the center.
4. Bring the top right corner to the center line.
5. Bring the top left corner to the center line.
6. Fold the bottom rectangular piece up.
7. Turn the hat over.
8. Fold the other bottom piece up.

Grammar notes   adjectives in a series
locative phrases
-ing phrase
-ed adjective (folded)

Follow up
1. After the operation is completed, practice using questions, such as: Where is the hat? How many times did you fold the paper? How did you make the hat?
2. Write an original operation explaining how to make something out of paper.

Making a Paper Airplane

Materials   sheets of paper

Key words
in half	point	fold
lengthwise	illustration	crease
edge	wing	
crease		

Operation

1. Fold a sheet of paper in half lengthwise.
2. Bring one top edge to the crease and fold.
3. Turn over and repeat on the other side.
4. Fold again, bringing point A to point B (see illustration), and crease.
5. Repeat on the other side.
6. Make a lengthwise fold to produce a wing.
7. Repeat on the other side.
8. Fly the airplane to test it.

Grammar notes   infinitive phrases
                    -ing phrase

Follow up
1. Have a contest to see whose airplane will fly the highest and the longest distance.
2. Rewrite the operation as a paragraph. Use transition words, such as first, second, then, next, and in addition.
3. Write a story about an airplane, such as An Airplane Crash or Brandon's First Flight.

Sharpening a Pencil

Materials pencils, a pencil sharpener, sheets of paper

Key words
end
hole
firmly
pencil sharpener

crank
sharp

turn
keep
try

Operation

1. Hold the pencil.
2. Put the end of the pencil into the hole.
3. Hold the pencil firmly in the pencil sharpener.
4. Turn the crank with your right hand.
5. Keep turning the crank until the pencil is sharp.
6. Take the pencil out of the pencil sharpener.
7. Look to see if it is sharp.
8. Try writing on a sheet of paper with it.

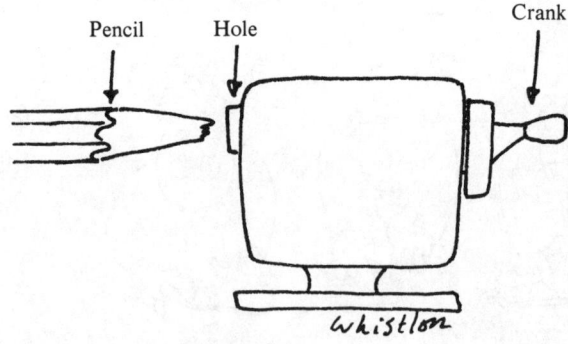

Grammar notes   -ing phrases
                  infinitive phrases
                  locative phrases
                  "until" clause
                  "if" clause

Follow up
1. After each step, Student A asks a *different* question. For example, "Where is the pencil? Where is the hole? How did you hold the pencil?" Student B answers the questions.
2. Student A gives directions and Student B follows them. When the operation is finished, Student A asks, "What did you do?" Student B explains the complete process in the past tense. Change roles and do it again.
3. Rewrite the operation adding adverbs to those steps that don't have any. For instance: Hold the pencil firmly.

HOUSEHOLD ACTIVITIES

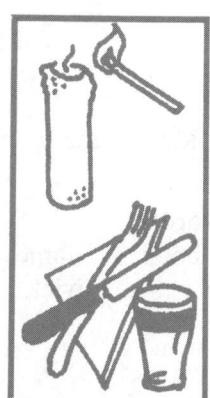
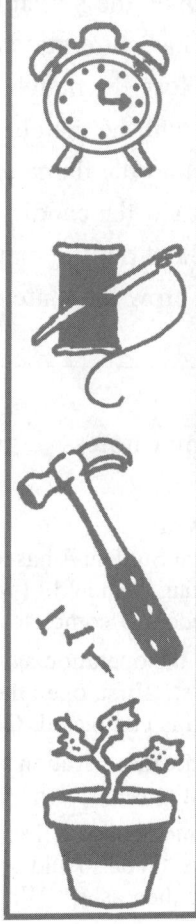

Lighting a Candle

Materials   match books or boxes, candles

Key words

match book	flame	tear out	blow out
candle	wick	light	throw away

Operation

1. Open the match book.
2. Tear out a match.
3. Close the match book.
4. Light the match.
5. Hold the flame to the candle wick.
6. Light the candle.
7. Blow out the match.
8. Throw the match away.

Grammar notes   two-word verbs

Follow up
1. After Student A has read each step, Student B checks his comprehension by asking, "Should I (*open the match book*)?" Student A answers, and then Student B completes the action.
2. Do the operation again and use ordinal numbers. For example, Student A says, "First, open the matchbook. Second. . . ." Continue until the operation is completed. Change roles.
3. Write the operation as a paragraph by combining some of the steps. Use the past tense.
4. Mime lighting a fire. Student A asks, "What should I do first?" Student B says, "You should open the match book." Student A opens the match book and then asks, "What do I do next?" Student B answers, and so on.

Setting a Table

Materials placemat, plate, teaspoon, knife, fork, glass, napkin

Key words

plate	napkin	fork	fold
center	knife	left-hand side	place
placemat	teaspoon		set

Operation

1. Put the plate in the center of the placemat.
2. Fold the napkin.
3. Put the napkin to the left of the plate.
4. Place the knife to the right of the plate.
5. Put the teaspoon to the right of the knife.
6. Put the fork on the left-hand side of the plate.
7. Set the glass above the knife.

Grammar notes   locative phrases

Follow up

1. Close your books. Student A completes the operation without interruption. He tells what he is doing *while* he is doing it. For example, "I'm putting the plate in the center of. . . ." Change roles.
2. Close your books. Student A completes the operation without interruption. Student B describes what he is doing, using as many tenses as he can. "He's putting the plate in the center of the placemat. Now he's going to. . . . He's just put it. . . ." and so on.
3. Complete the following story: Sherman lost his glasses last night, and he had a lot of trouble setting the table. He put the napkin under the plate. He put the fork. . . ."

Setting an Alarm Clock

Materials   alarm clock

Key words
alarm clock	alarm hand	wind	ring
hour hand	alarm button	set	push in
minute hand		pull out	

Operation

1. Wind the alarm clock.
2. Set the hour and minute hand at the correct time.
3. Set the alarm hand for 7:00.
4. Pull out the alarm button.
5. When the alarm rings, push in the alarm button.
6. Get out of bed.

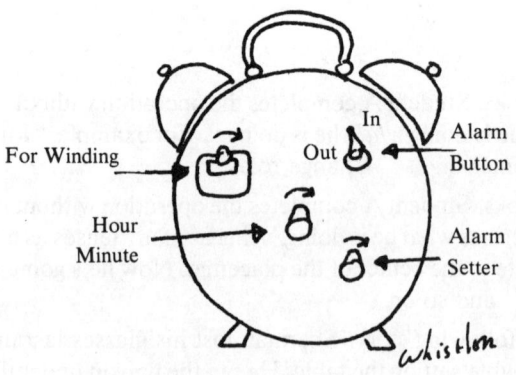

Grammar notes   compound nouns
two-word verbs
verbs that take particular prepositions
(set at, set for)

Follow up
1. Write five questions that relate to the operation, such as: Why do you use an alarm clock? When do you get up? Then ask another student your questions. When finished, change roles.
2. Complete the following story: Jennifer is always late for class in the morning. She tells her teacher that she is late because she doesn't have an alarm clock. Finally Jennifer buys an alarm clock, but she doesn't know how to use it. Her friend Eleanor says, "I'll tell you how to use an alarm clock. First, you. . . ."

Threading a Needle

Materials a needle, some thread, some buttons

Key words
needle   thread   knotted   moisten
thumb   eye   knot   tie

Operation

1. Hold the needle between your thumb and first finger.
2. Hold the thread in your other hand.
3. Moisten one end of the thread with your mouth.
4. Put the thread through the eye of the needle.
5. Pull the thread through.
6. Tie a knot in one end of the thread.
7. Make the knotted end longer than the other end.

Grammar notes locative phrases
comparatives (longer than)
possessive pronouns used with parts of the body
the use of "one" and "other"
-ed adjective

Follow up
1. Student A gives directions and Student B follows them. When the operation is completed, Student A asks, "What did you do?" Student B explains the complete process in the past tense. Change roles and do it again.
2. Complete the following story: Mrs. Anderson is teaching her son how to thread a needle. He soon will leave for college and she wants him to be able to mend his clothes and sew on buttons. She says, "First, you hold the needle...."
3. Invent an operation for sewing on a button. Divide into pairs and practice it.

Sewing On a Button

Materials   buttons, needles, fabric, thread

Key words
needle   fabric   sew
knot   hole   thread
thread   tightly   tie
button   cut

Operation

1. Thread the needle.
2. Tie a knot in the end of the thread.
3. Hold the button on the fabric.
4. Pull the needle through the fabric and through one of the holes in the button.
5. Bring the needle back through another hole.
6. Repeat until the button is on tightly.
7. Tie a knot in the thread.
8. Cut the thread.

Grammar notes   locative phrases
                    "until" clause

Follow up
1. Do the operation again and make the statements more polite by adding modal auxiliaries and polite expressions. For example, "*Would you please* thread the needle? *Good, next you can* tie a knot in the end...."
2. Rewrite the operation, adding a descriptive adjective to each step.
3. Discuss male and female sex roles in various cultures. In what cultures is it considered improper for a man to sew on a button?

Pounding a Nail

Materials   nails, a hammer, wood

Key words

nail	end	sharp	pick up	remove
thumb	handle	secure	hold	continue
finger	wood		hit	
hammer	head			

Operation

1. Pick up the nail with one hand.
2. Hold it between your thumb and first finger.
3. Pick up the hammer with your other hand.
4. Hold it at the end of its handle.
5. Put the sharp end of the nail against the wood.
6. Hit the head of the nail with the hammer.
7. Remove your fingers when the nail is secure.
8. Continue hitting the head until the nail is hammered into the wood.

Grammar notes   locative phrases
"of" phrases showing possession
  (of its handle, of the nail)
time clauses (until, when)
possessive adjectives
passive voice

Follow up
1. Rewrite the operation and add an adverb to each step. Try to use eight different adverbs.
2. Write a story about a clumsy carpenter.

Potting a Plant

Materials   a pot, some soil, small stones, water

Key words

stones	gently	pot
pot	firmly	press
soil	carefully	fill up
plant	slowly	water
excess	half full	drain

Operation

1. Put some stones gently into the pot.
2. Fill the pot half full with soil.
3. Place the plant firmly into the soil.
4. Fill the pot up carefully with soil.
5. Press the soil firmly around the plant.
6. Water the plant slowly.
7. Let the excess water drain out of the pot.

Grammar notes   adverbs of manner
locative phrases
count and noncount nouns
shift from no article to the definite article

Follow up
1. Do it as a dictation. Student A reads the operation to Student B. Student B writes down what Student A says. After you're finished, check your work with your book. Change roles and do it again.
2. Write the operation in narrative form in the past tense. For example, "Yesterday Jeffrey potted a plant. He put some stones gently into the pot and filled. . . ."

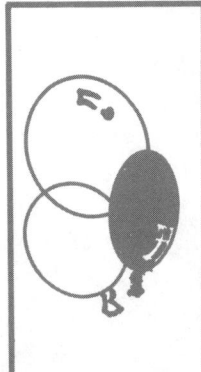

GAMES AND EXERCISES

Touching Your Toes

Materials   none

Key words
apart   knees   place   touch
waist   straight   raise up   keep
                        bend down   return

Operation

1. Stand up.
2. Place your feet a foot apart.
3. Raise your arms up over your head.
4. Bend down from the waist.
5. Touch your toes with your fingers.
6. Keep your knees straight.
7. Return to a standing position.

Grammar notes   possessive pronouns used with parts of the body
two-word verbs
locative phrases
-ing adjective

Follow up
1. After you complete the operation, write five questions that relate to it, such as: Where were your feet? Did you keep your knees straight? Then, ask your partner the questions. Your partner answers the questions and then asks his questions.
2. Write an operation on doing sit-ups. Perform the operation in pairs.
3. Write an operation on another keep-fit exercise. Perform it in pairs.

Hopping On One Leg

Materials   none

Key words

ankle	times	bend	hop
balance		grab	let go
		concentrate	keep

Operation

1. Stand on both feet.
2. Bend your left knee.
3. Raise your left foot behind you.
4. Grab your left ankle with your left hand.
5. Concentrate on keeping your balance.
6. Hop five times.
7. Let go of your ankle.
8. Put your foot on the floor.

Grammar notes   locative phrases
possessive pronouns used with parts of the body
-ing phrase

Follow up

1. Do the operation again, and add transition words and phrases. For example, "*First* stand on both feet. *Now* bend your left knee. *OK, next you're ready to* raise. . . ."
2. Student A writes each step of the operation on a separate piece of paper, and then mixes the pieces up and gives them to Student B. Student B puts the steps in their correct order and then reads them to Student A. Student A follows the directions.

Blowing Up a Balloon

Materials balloons

Key words
balloon	full	stretch	escape
end	knot	blow (up)	tie

Operation

1. Stretch the balloon.
2. Put the open end into your mouth.
3. Blow into the balloon until it's full.
4. Take it out of your mouth.
5. Hold the end together so that the air doesn't escape.
6. Tie a knot in the end of the balloon.

Grammar notes   locative phrases
"until" clause
"so that" clause
formation of negatives
contractions

Follow up
1. Close your books. Student A gives the directions as well as he is able. When the operation is completed, Student A asks, "What did you do?" Student B explains the process. Change roles and do it again.
2. Rewrite the operation, adding a different adverb to each step.
3. Rewrite the operation in narrative form, and finish the following story: Tomorrow Connie is going to a birthday party. At the party she will blow up a balloon. . . .

Playing Jacks

Materials   jacks, a small rubber ball

Key words
jacks throw bounce repeat
one at a time toss catch

Operation

1. Throw the jacks onto the floor.
2. Toss the ball into the air.
3. Pick up one jack before the ball bounces.
4. Let the ball bounce once.
5. Catch the ball with the same hand.
6. Put the jack into your other hand.
7. Repeat until you've picked up all the jacks, one at a time.

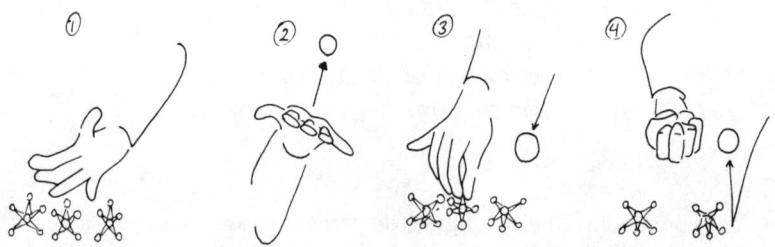

Grammar notes   time clauses (before, until)
                 locative phrases
                 "let" + noun phrase + bare infinitive
                 use of "one" and "other"

Follow up
1. Do it as a dictation. Student A reads the operation to Student B. Student B writes down what Student A says. After you're finished, check your work with your text. Change roles and do it again.
2. Close your books. Student A completes the operation. He tells what he is doing *while* he is doing it. When he's finished, Student B completes the operation in the same way.
3. Close your books. Student A completes the operation. Student B describes what he is doing while he is doing it. He uses as many tenses as he can. For instance: "She is throwing the jacks onto the floor. Now she's just. . . . She's going to . . . ," and so on.

Relaxation Breathing

Materials   none

Key words

relaxation	several	inhale	repeat
straight	times	exhale	concentrate
lap	counting		
silently	breathing		

Operation

1. Sit up straight in your chair.
2. Close your eyes.
3. Put your hands in your lap.
4. Slowly inhale while counting silently from one to six.
5. Slowly exhale while counting silently from one to six.
6. Repeat several times.
7. Concentrate on your breathing.
8. Think only about your breathing and counting.

Grammar notes   possessive pronouns
adverbs of manner (slowly, straight, silently)
"while" clauses
-ing phrases

Follow up

1. Student A gives the directions, and Student B follows them. When the operation is completed, Student A asks, "What did you do?" Student B explains the complete process as well as he is able. Change roles and do it again.
2. Practice using additional questions, such as: Where did you sit? How did you inhale? Where were your hands? How many times did you inhale?

Playing Dice

Score Sheet

2	
3	
4	
5	
6	
7	
8	
9	
10	
11	
12	

(To be played in groups of 2 or 3)

Materials dice

Key words
score sheet   player   count
dice   steps   check
dots
check mark

Operation

1. Pick up two dice.
2. Throw the dice on top of the desk.
3. Count the number of dots on top of the dice.
4. Put a check mark after the same number on the score sheet.
5. Give the dice to the next player.
6. Tell him to do steps one through six.
7. Continue until you have checked all the numbers.

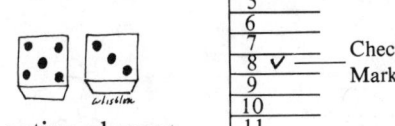
Check Mark

Grammar notes   locative phrases
verbs that take particular prepositions
   (get from, give to)
compound nouns
"until" clause

Follow up
1. Write an operation on playing a different game of dice.
2. Write a story titled "Johnny, the Gambler."

Playing Concentration with Cards

(To be played in groups of 2, 3, 4, or 5)

Materials   decks of cards

Key words
card   face down   turn up   complete
location   steps   remember   turn down

Operation

1. Lay each card face down.
2. Turn one card up.
3. Turn another card up.
4. If the numbers are alike, take both cards.
5. If the numbers are different, turn both cards down.
6. Remember the location of the cards.
7. Let the other player complete steps 1 through 5.
8. Continue until all the cards are paired.

Grammar notes   two-word verbs
"if" clauses
comparative adjectives
use of "one," "another," and "other"
"let" + bare infinitive

Follow up
1. Write a paragraph titled "How to Play Concentration."
2. Make a concentration game for matching verb forms, two-word verbs and their definitions, or idioms and their definitions. Then, play the game.

Playing War

(To be played in groups of 2 or 3, each group using 1 deck of cards)

Materials   several decks of cards

Key words
deck of cards   tie   shuffle
face up   steps   deal
in case of

Operation

1. Shuffle the deck of cards.
2. Deal the other player one card face up.
3. Deal yourself one card face up.
4. If you have the higher card, take both cards.
5. If you have the lower card, give both cards to the other player.
6. In case of a tie, deal two more cards and repeat steps 4 and 5.
7. Continue until all the cards have been played.

Grammar notes "if" clauses
comparative forms of adjectives (higher, lower)
quantifiers "both," "all," and "two"
"until" clause
passive voice

Follow up
1. Divide into groups of three. Student A gives the directions, and Students B and C play the game. When the game is over, Student A asks, "What did you do?" Students B and C tell him what they did.
2. Write an operation on playing a card game. Teach someone the game, using the operation.
3. Write an operation on building a house of cards. Divide into pairs. Student A tells Student B what to do. See which pair can make the tallest card house.

FOOD AND RECIPES

Eating Cookies

Materials   a box of cookies in a bag

Key words
bag   cookie   take out
box   another   eat

Operation

1. Take the bag.
2. Open the bag.
3. Take out the box.
4. Open the box.
5. Take a cookie.
6. Eat the cookie.
7. Take another one.
8. Close the box.

Grammar notes   the use of "one" as a noun substitute
shift from "a" to "the"

Follow up
1. Close your books and sit in a circle. Pass the bag of cookies around the circle. Each student says the operation to the student next to him. Continue until the bag of cookies has been passed completely around the circle.

Eating an Apple

Materials   apples, water, towels, knives

Key words

apple	mouth	wash	bite
dry	teeth	wipe	chew
red	core	hold	swallow

Operation

1. Wash the apple.
2. Wipe it dry.
3. Hold it in your hand.
4. Open your mouth.
5. Put the apple between your teeth.
6. Bite into it.
7. Take the apple away from your mouth.
8. Chew and swallow.

Grammar notes   locative phrases
the object pronoun "it"
possessives used with parts of the body

Follow up
1. Rewrite the operation, and add a descriptive adjective to steps 1, 3, 4, 5, and 7.
2. Write an operation on eating a banana.
3. Write an operation on peeling an apple. Divide into pairs and perform the operation. Try to peel it so that the peel comes off in one unbroken strip.
4. Write an operation for cutting up the apple and taking out the core. Perform the operation in pairs.

Making a Cup of Coffee

Materials instant coffee, cups, spoons, milk, sugar, water, percolator or hot plate.

Key words
coffee	milk	boil	stir
cup	sugar	fill	add
boiling			

Operation

1. Boil some water.
2. Put some coffee into your cup.
3. Fill the cup with boiling water.
4. Stir the coffee.
5. Add some milk to the coffee.
6. Add some sugar.
7. Stir the coffee again.

Grammar notes count and noncount nouns
the use of "some" and "the"
verbs that take particular prepositions
   (add to, fill with)
-ing adjective

Follow up
1. Close your books. As Student A completes the operation, Student B describes what Student A is doing. For example, "You're boiling some water. Now, you're putting some coffee...."
2. Close your books. While Student A performs the operation, Student B talks about what Student A is doing, using as many tenses as he can. For example, "He's just put the water into.... Soon the water will.... Now he's...."
3. Write an operation on making tea.

Making Instant Pudding

Materials   a package of instant pudding, milk, a bowl, spoons, serving bowls

Key words
directions   mixture   pour   allow
package   bowl   stir   thicken
contents   pudding
amount

Operation

1. Read the directions on the package.
2. Open the package and pour the contents into a bowl.
3. Add the correct amount of milk.
4. Stir the mixture together.
5. Pour it into individual bowls.
6. Allow it to thicken.
7. Eat it.

Grammar notes   the object pronoun "it"
          locative phrases
          compound verb

Follow up
1. Do it as a dictation. Student A reads the operation to Student B. Student B writes down what Student A says. After you're finished, check your work with your book. Change roles and do it again.
2. Discuss the American measurement system (cup, teaspoon, etc.).
3. Discuss other American "instant" or "fast" foods.

Making a Peanut Butter and Jelly Sandwich

Materials a loaf of bread, a jar of peanut butter, a jar of jelly, a knife

Key words
slice	jar	unscrew
package	jelly	spread
lid	sandwich	screw
peanut butter	in half	

Operation

1. Take two slices of bread from the package.
2. Unscrew the lid of the peanut butter jar.
3. Unscrew the lid of the jelly jar.
4. Spread the peanut butter on one slice of bread.
5. Spread the jelly on the other slice of bread.
6. Put the two slices of bread together.
7. Cut the sandwich in half.
8. Screw the lids on the jars.

Grammar notes count and noncount nouns
"of" phrases showing possession
use of "one" and "other"

Follow up
1. Student A writes each step of the operation on a separate piece of paper. Then, he mixes them up and gives them to Student B. Student B puts the steps in their correct order and reads them to Student A. Student A follows the directions.
2. Write a recipe in the form of an operation.

COMMUNICATION

Mailing a Letter

Materials   paper, envelopes, pens, stamps

Key words
letter	upper	fold
envelope	left-hand	lick
flap	corner	seal
address	stamp	mail
front	right-hand	
return address		

Operation

1. Fold the letter to fit the envelope.
2. Put the letter in the envelope.
3. Lick the flap and seal the envelope.
4. Write the address on the front of the envelope.
5. Write the return address in the upper left-hand corner.
6. Lick the stamp.
7. Put the stamp in the upper right-hand corner.
8. Mail the letter.

Grammar notes   locative phrases
infinitive phrase used as an adverb of manner (to fit)

Follow up
1. Divide into pairs and sit back to back. Student A gives Student B directions for drawing and addressing an envelope. Student A follows the directions that he gives Student B, so that both students are drawing the same thing. Student A should be as detailed and specific as possible. For example, Student A says, "Draw an envelope that is 4 by 9 inches. In the upper right-hand corner, draw a. . . ." Both students follow the directions. Student B may ask questions but may not see Student A's picture until it is finished. When finished, compare pictures. Change roles and do it again.
2. Write a letter to an American who knows nothing about your country.

Using a Pay Telephone

Materials   a telephone (or a drawing of one), some coins

Key words
directions
telephone receiver
dial tone
continuous
hole
desired
pay telephone
pick up
insert
dial

Operation

1. Read the directions.
2. Pick up the telephone receiver.
3. Hold it to your ear.
4. Insert the correct amount of money.
5. Listen for the dial tone, a continuous sound.
6. Put your finger in the hole and dial the desired number.
7. Listen until someone answers on the other end.

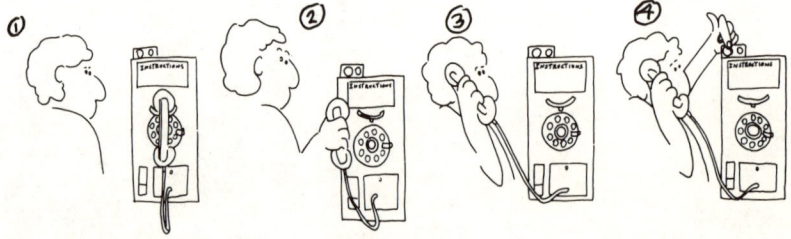

Grammar notes   noun in apposition
                 -ed adjective (desired)
                 compound nouns
                 "until" clause

Follow up
1. Write this operation as a paragraph adding five adjective clauses to the first operation. Example: First, you read the directions that are near the telephone. . . .
2. Write an operation on making a long-distance phone call.
3. Write an operation on sending a telegram by phone. Divide into pairs. Perform the operation. Student A dictates the message, and Student B writes it down. Compare the messages. Then reverse roles.

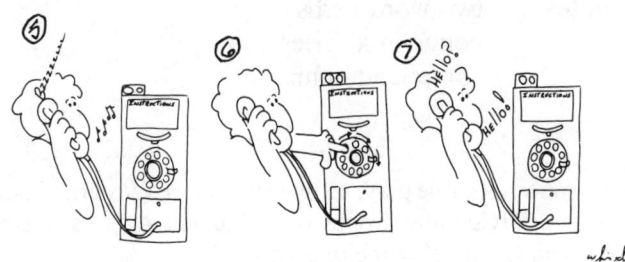

Sending a Telegram

Materials   a telephone book

Key words
Western Union   clearly   look up
phone book   message   write down
telegram form   bottom   print

Operation
1. Look up Western Union in the phone book.
2. Write down the address.
3. Go to the Western Union office.
4. Ask for a telegram form.
5. Print the name and address clearly on the form.
6. In as few words as possible, print your message.
7. Print your name, address, and phone number at the bottom of the form.
8. Pay the person the correct amount of money.

Grammar notes   two-word verbs
nouns in a series
compound nouns

Follow up
1. Do this operation as a role play, setting up a mock Western Union office in the classroom. Divide into groups of 3; Student A gives directions, and Students B and C role play the operation.
2. The Telegram Game: Divide into pairs. Student A is the parent and Student B is the child. Student B is away from home at a special summer camp, and she is out of money. She writes a telegram to the parent asking for money. The parent refuses. The parent and the child can exchange as many telegrams as they want, but they cannot exceed a 100-word total for all telegrams. The object for Student B is to convince the parent to send the

money. The object for Student A is to make up excuses not to send the money.

For example: Student B writes, "Send money."
Student A writes, "Why?"
Student B writes, "Want to buy a horse."
Etc.

Wiring Money

Materials   a telephone book

Key words
Western Union   clearly   look up
phone book   carefully   write down
money order form   charge   fill in
                                       wire

Operation

1. Look up Western Union in the phone book.
2. Write down the address.
3. Go to the Western Union office with the cash that you want to send.
4. Tell the person that you want to wire money.
5. Fill in the money order form.
6. Print clearly and carefully.
7. Give the person the money that you're sending.
8. Pay the charge for sending the money.

Grammar notes   two-word verbs
adverbs of manner (clearly, carefully)
"that" clauses used as noun clause
   and relative clause
compound nouns
double object verbs (tell, give)

Follow up
1. Do this operation as a role play, setting up a mock Western Union office in the classroom. Divide into groups of 3; Student A gives directions, and Students B and C role play the operation. When completed, change roles and do it again.
2. Call Western Union and find out what other services they offer. Compare these services with those offered by telephone companies in other countries.

SEE IMPORTANT INFORMATION ON THE REVERSE SIDE OF THIS FORM. PRESS FIRMLY - PRINT CLEARLY.

western union
Telegraphic Money Order Application

SENDING DATA	CLASS TYPE	OFFICE	WORD COUNT	DATE AND FILING TIME	CLERK'S INIT. AND ACCT'G. INFORMATION

MOD ⬜⬜⬜⬜

88 688

↙ DO NOT WRITE ABOVE THIS LINE ↘

$ | AMT.
  | FEE
S | TOLLS
  | RP MGM
E | TAX
  | TOTAL

PAY AMOUNT: _____ /100 DOLLARS (_____)
                                  FIGURES

TO: _____
    ☐ REPORT PAYMENT BY MAILGRAM
      (ADDITIONAL CHARGE)

CAU OR VIG
YES ☐ NO ☐

TEST QUESTION: _____
STREET ADDRESS
AND APT. NUMBER: _____ TELEPHONE NO. _____
                CITY: _____ STATE: _____ ZIP: _____

SENDER'S NAME: _____
SENDER'S STREET
ADDRESS AND APT. NO.: _____
                CITY: _____ STATE: _____ ZIP: _____
                (IF REPORT PAYMENT REQUESTED)

MESSAGE: _____

= MOD =

EOM (_____ / _____ / _____)   ⌐CS) . X-OFF
      (SENDER'S NAME) (ADDRESS)   (CITY-STATE-ZIP)   (TELEPHONE NO.)

● Unless signed below the Telegraph Company is directed to pay this
  money order at my risk to such person as its paying agent believes
  to be the above named payee, personal identification being waived.
  Foreign money orders excepted.

W.U. 72
(R12-77)

⑈"090688 50"⑈ 66

MISCELLANY

Writing a Check

Materials   pens or pencils

Key words
check   amount   sign
date line   figures
payee

Operation

1. Write today's date on the date line.
2. Write the payee's name on the next line.
3. Write the amount of the check in figures.
4. Write the amount of the check in words.
5. Sign the check on the last line.

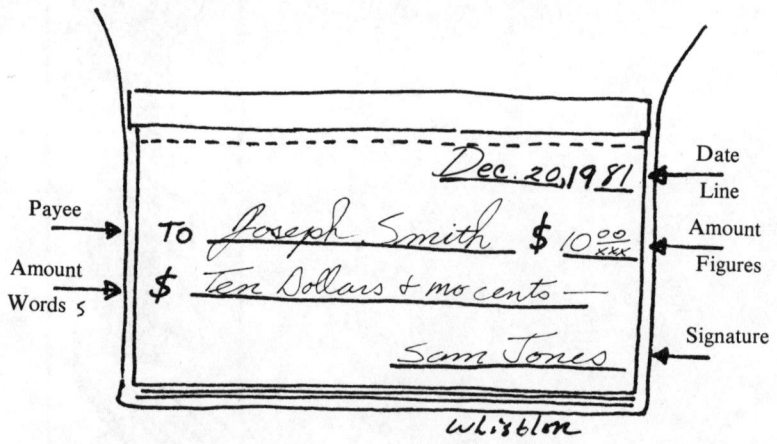

Grammar notes   locative phrases
possessives (steps 1, 2) vs. genitive "of" phrases (steps 3, 4)

Follow up
1. Write five questions that relate to the operation, such as: What is the date? Where did you sign the check? Then, ask another student the questions. When finished, change roles.
2. Combine the complete operation into one sentence using as few words as possible.
3. Write the complete operation in two sentences, using the words "after" and "before."

Opening a Pull-Top Can

Materials   an unopened pull-top can of soda

Key words
pull-top
firmly
index finger
straight up
motion
wastebasket
pull
throw

Operation

1. Hold the can firmly in one hand.
2. Put your index finger through the pull-top.
3. Pull the top straight up in one motion.
4. Throw the top into the wastebasket.
5. Drink it.

Grammar notes   locative phrases
                      prepositional phrases of manner

Follow up
1. Do it as a dictation. Student A reads the operation to Student B. Student B writes down what Student A says. After you're finished, check your work with your book. Change roles and do it again.
2. Write an operation on opening a jar or a pop bottle.

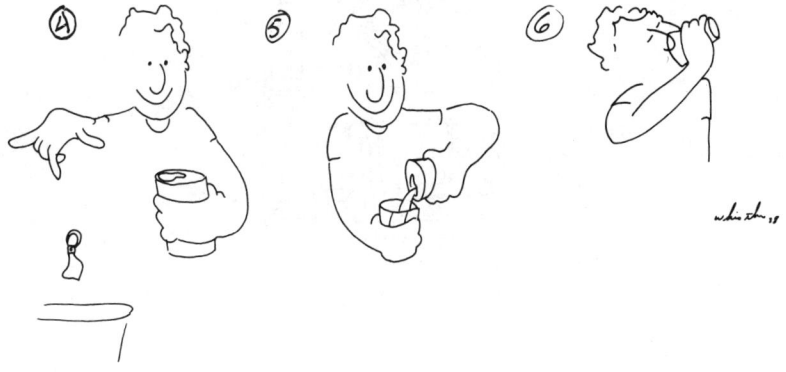

Using a Vending Machine

Materials   a vending machine (or a picture of one), coins

Key words

vending machine	button	select
directions	knob	push
coin slot	selection	want
exact change		buy

Operation

1. Read the directions on the vending machine.
2. Select what you want to buy.
3. Find the coin slot.
4. Put the exact change into the coin slot.
5. Push the button, open the door, or pull the knob.
6. Take your selection from the machine.

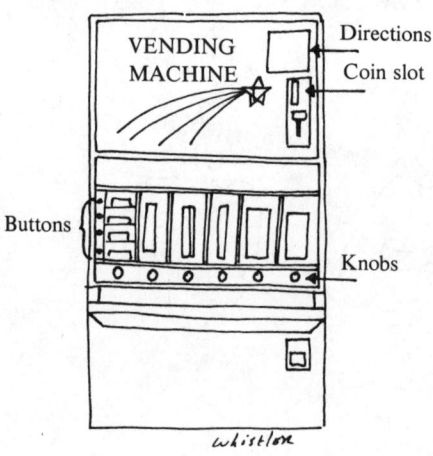

Grammar notes   locative phrases
compound nouns
verbs joined by "or"

Follow up
1. Write five questions that relate to the operation, such as: What did you buy? Where is the coin slot? Then ask another student your questions. That student replies to the questions. When finished, change roles.
2. List all the different things that are sold in vending machines. Discuss vending machines and American culture (fast foods and junk foods).

Finding an Apartment

Materials   a newspaper (optional)

Key words

apartment	rent	consider
Want Ads	listings	select
furnished	features	call
unfurnished	available	
section	arrangements	
heading	apts.	

Operation

1. Look at the Want Ads.
2. Find the sections headed "Furnished Apts." and "Unfurnished Apts."
3. Read the listings in those sections.
4. Consider the size, location, features, condition, and rent.
5. Select an apartment and call the number in the listing.
6. Ask questions about the apartment.
7. Ask if the apartment is still available.
8. If so, make arrangements to see it.

Grammar notes   infinitive phrase
nouns in a series

Follow up

1. Write a telephone dialog between a landlord and a prospective tenant. Role play the dialog.
2. Write down the abbreviations from the Want Ads (RMS, BR, A/C, etc.), and find out their meanings.
3. Write an operation for choosing a secondhand automobile from newspaper ads, and telephoning the person who wishes to sell. Role play the situation. The automobile is in bad condition. Student A, who wants to buy, tries to discover the truth. Student B, who wants to sell, tries to hide it.

WANT ADS

60. Furnished Apts. 60.

3rd FLOOR apt., renovated by June 1, avail. May 21, close in, $130, utils. included, carpeted, all conveniences, no pets. Prefer working man, grad student or working student. Call before 10 a.m. or after 6 p.m., 296-3396. a (T5-26)

1 BR MASONRY Construction Apartments Available in Star City. Completely Furnished, W/W Carpeting, Air-Conditioning, 2 Large Double Closets, Located within five minutes of walking to shopping facilities. Lease & Deposit Required. ERA Mountaineer Realty 599-2333 ask for Debbie. (T5-22)

3 ROOMS & BATH $200 mo. includes utilities, deposit & lease required, no pets. Ph. after 5, 291-1223. (T5-26)

1 BR. Efficiency Apt. $140. utils pd. plus dep., Male only. 1 BR Apt. $225 plus dep., Couple only. Free TV & parking. 292-4532, 11-5 p.m. 292-3039 after 7 p.m. (T5-25)

CHEAT ROAD APTS. - Efficiency $165; 3 Rooms & Bath $190; 4 Rooms & Bath $200. You Pay Electric & Deposit. Call 292-0617. (T5-23)

NICELY FURN. 2 BR Apt. Located Close to Downtown. All Utilities Furn. (Westover). $375/Month. Lease & Deposit. 599-6351 or 599-4029. (T5-14TF)

EFFICIENCY APARTMENT FOR RENT, also 1 BEDROOM APARTMENT FOR RENT. PHONE 599-2319. (T5-14TF)

MODERN 2 BR, A/C, Hot Water Heat, Nicely Furn. Westover Plaza Apts. $295/Mo. Includes all Utilities. No Children or Pets. Lease & Deposit. 296-3704 or 296-9327 or 291-9042. (T6-14)

FURN. EFFICIENCY APT. Available June 1st. Located in Westover. $150/Mo. Plus Util. Cozy - Ideal for Elderly Individual. For Inform. Call 292-1421 Days, 291-6590 Eves. (T5-29)

3 LG. RMS. Suitable for Cple. or 2 Students. Close Campus. $250/Mo. Plus Elec. Deposit, Lease, No Pets. Call 292-8366. (T5-21)

2 STUDENT APTS.
Campus Area & North Hills For Summer & Fall. Call 598-0321. (T6-10)

61. Unfurnished Apts. 61.

FOR RENT: 6 BR unfurnished Apartment. ½ block from WVU Library. Girls only. Inquire 174 Willey St. (T5-10tf)

1 BR APT. Available June 1st. Carport, A/C, 5 Min. Walk to Town. Mrd. Cple. or Single Working Person. 291-2357 or 292-5094. (T5-24)

GRAFTON ROAD: Miles out. New 2 BR Apts., Kit. Furn., Carpeted, $275/Mo. plus Deposit & Elec. 1 Child, No Pets 292 2523 or 292-8828 after 5 PM. (T6-2)

MODERN APT. in WO, W-W carpet, 2 BR, electric range, refrig., DW, central A/C, $225 mo. plus utils, lease & deposit. No pets, walking distance to downtown, avail. June 1, 292-1337. (T5-21)

APT. FOR SUBLET - Bon Vista. 2 BR Avail. June 1st., $250/Month Call 599-6876 after 5 PM (T5 25)

2 BR APARTMENTS
Available Now, No pets
Ph. 292-7947 after 5 or 296-4468, ask for Dale (T5-21)

2nd FLOOR - 3 BR Apt. Available in Sunnyside Location. $285/Per Month Including Utilities. Call Dave & Stacy after 5 - 296-8820. (T5-24)

MODERN 2 BR Apt. Avail. June 1st, W/W carpet, A/C, Washer/Dryer hook-up. 5 min. walk to Med Ctr. Ph. 599-4583. (T5-22)

2 BR, Recently remodeled. Located WO. $175 plus gas & electric. Lease & Deposit. Ph. 292-9439. (T5-17tf)

NEW Townhouses now under construction. 2 BR, Bath 2, Drapes, Carpet Throughout, Complete Built-In Kitchen, Garage. N. West Dr. Within Walking Distance to Med Center. Lease & Deposit Required. Call 599-4988. (T5-17TF)

3 BR, Combined Kitchen/DR/LR. Also 2 BR Apt. with Efficiency Kit. Write PO Box 779, Morgantown, (T6-13)

Using a Map

Materials   paper, pencil, map (optional)

Key words
map	index	find out
symbols	index reference system	write down
scale	approximate	figure out

Operation

1. Place the map so that north is at the top.
2. Find out the name of the map.
3. Write down the map symbols and their meanings.
4. Look at the scale of the map.
5. Find the city of Brattleboro in the index.
6. Write down the letter and number that follow it.
7. Using the index reference system, locate Brattleboro on the map.
8. Figure out the approximate distance between Burlington and Montpelier.

Grammar notes   two-word verbs
"so that" clause

Follow up
1. Rewrite the operation in narrative form in the past tense. For example, "Barbara wanted to go to Brattleboro, Vermont, so she got a map. She placed the map...."
2. Bring in a road map and plan a trip, including what roads to use, where to spend the night, and what places to visit. Discuss your trip with a partner or in a small group.
3. Bring in two road maps of a city. Divide into pairs and sit back to back. Imagine each pair is in an automobile. Student A is driving and Student B reads the map and gives directions on the route to follow. For example: "Turn right at the corner of Oak Street and First Avenue. Take the next left turn." As Student B gives directions, he marks the route with a pencil. As Student A follows directions, he marks the route with a pencil. At the end of the journey, compare the two maps and see if the routes are the same. Reverse roles and choose a new route.

A ROAD MAP OF VERMONT

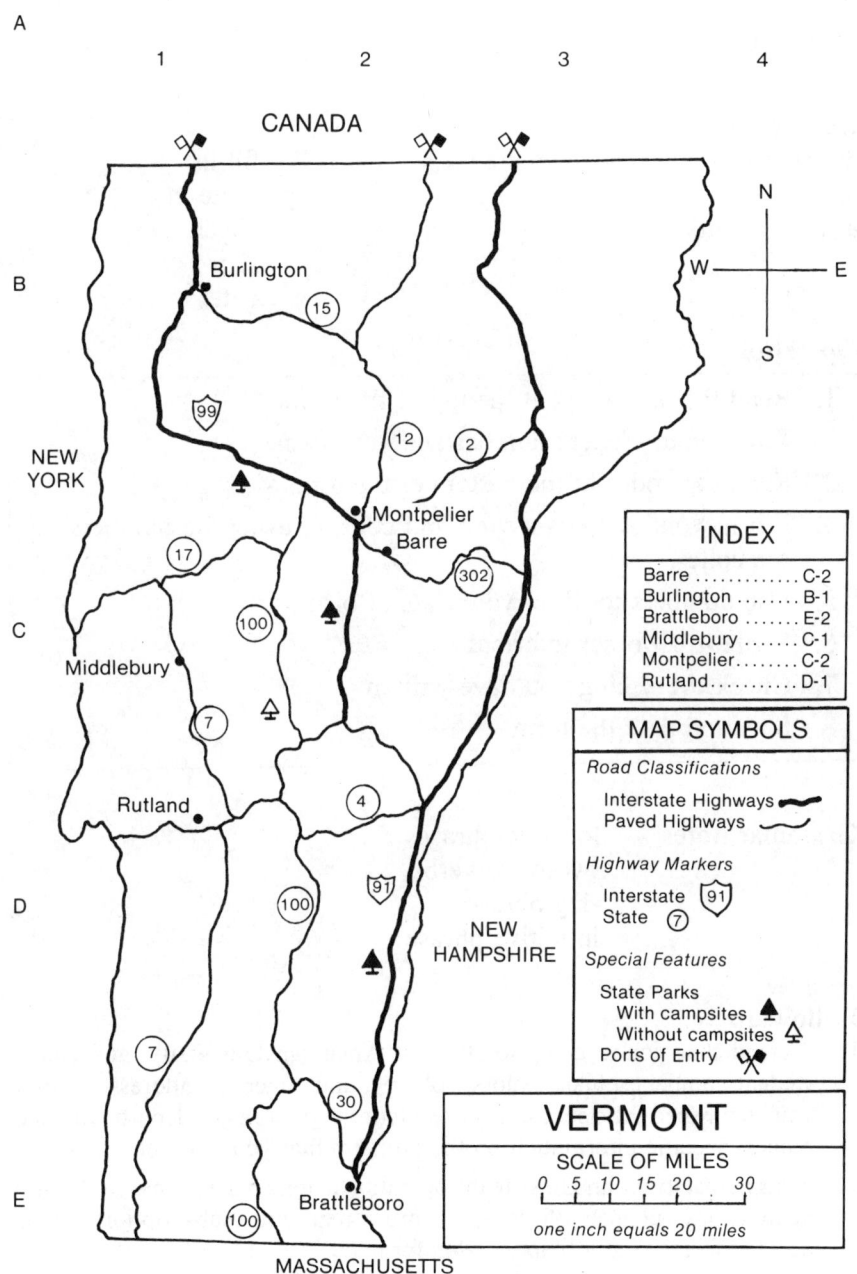

Filling in a Form

Materials pens or pencils

Key words
directions   academic college   fill in
code   form   write in
academic rank   check
                                                sign
                                                date

Operation

1. Read the directions at the top of the form.
2. Fill in your student number and your name.
3. Read the codes at the bottom of the form.
4. Fill in your academic rank and college, using the numbers in the codes.
5. Use numbers to fill in your date of birth.
6. Write in all other information.
7. Check everything you have written.
8. Sign and date the form.

Grammar notes   locative phrases
                    two-word verbs
                    -ing phrase
                    infinitive phrase

Follow up
1. Pretend that you're going to study at American University, and create student numbers, ranks, majors, colleges, and American addresses. After you've finished the operation, write a letter to your major department, and request specific information on the program that you're enrolling in.
2. Bring in real forms and rewrite the operation to match the forms (credit card applications, change of address cards, magazine subscriptions, bank account forms, and job application forms).

AMERICAN UNIVERSITY   Admissions and Records Center

STUDENT INFORMATION FORM

Read these directions first!
1. Print data in the appropriate blocks in each box.
2. Use the codes below when coded information is required.
3. Do not go beyond the number of blocks provided (abbreviate if necessary)

Student Number	Student Name (last, first)

Academic Rank (use code below)	Current Major	Academic College (see code below)	Sex F=female M=male

Marital Status M=married S=single	Date of birth mo. day year	Local Street Address

Local City Address	State	Zip Code

Student's Signature   Date

Rank Codes

Code	Rank
01	Freshman
02	Sophomore
03	Junior
04	Senior
05	Graduate Student

Schools and Colleges

Code	School or College
07	Agriculture and Forestry
14	Arts and Sciences
21	Business and Economics
35	Engineering
42	Graduate
45	Education
80	Dentistry
83	Medicine
86	Nursing

Note: A *major* area of study is in a department within a *college*; for example, a history major is in the College of Arts and Sciences; and a business administration major is in the College of Business and Economics

Key Verb Index
(These verbs are listed as key words.)

add 14, 57
advance 19
allow 58

bend 42
bend down 41
bite 56
blow (up) 43
blow out 28
boil 57
bounce 44
bring 20
buy 78

call 80
catch 44
check 47, 84
chew 56
color 13
complete 48
concentrate 42, 46
consider 80
continue 36
count 47
crease 22
cut 34

date 84
deal 50
dial 66
divide 14
do 13
drain 38
draw 12

eat 55
eject 19
erase 15
escape 43
exhale 46

fall 18
figure out 82
fill 57
fill in 70, 84
fill up 38
find 17
find out 82
fold 20, 22, 29, 64
follow 16

grab 42

hit 36
hold 15, 36, 56
hop 42

inhale 46
insert 19, 66

keep 24, 41, 42

let go 42
lick 64
light 28
look at 18
look for 17
look up 68, 70

mail 64
moisten 32
multiply 14

pick out 16
pick up 15, 36, 66
place 29, 41
play 19
plug in 19
pot 38
pour 58
press 38
print 68
pull 76
pull out 30
push 78
push in 30

raise up 41
record 19
release 19
remember 14, 48
remove 36
repeat 44, 46
return 41
rewind 19
ring 30

screw 60
seal 64
see 17
select 78, 80
set 29, 30
sew 34

shuffle 50
sign 74, 84
spread 60
stir 57, 58
stretch 43
subtract 14
swallow 56

take out 55
tear out 28
thicken 58
thread 34
throw 44, 76
throw away 28
tie 32, 34, 43
toss 44
touch 41
try 24
turn 24
turn down 48
turn to 16
turn up 48

unfold 20
unscrew 60

want 78
wash 56
water 38
wind 30
wipe 56
wire 70
write down 68, 70, 82
write in 84

Grammar Notes Index

Adjectives
    "another" 49
    articles: shift from "a" to "the" 13, 55
                  shift from no article to "the" 38
                  use of "some" and "the" 57
    comparatives 33, 49, 51
    definite and indefinite 12
    -ed adjectives 21, 33, 67
    -ing adjectives 41, 57
    "one" 33, 44, 49, 61
    ordinals 18
    "other" 33, 44, 49, 61
    possessive adjectives 37
    quantifiers 51
    series 21

Adverbs 38, 46, 65, 70

Clauses
    "if" clauses 18, 25, 49, 50
    "so that" clause 43, 82
    "that" clauses: as noun clauses 16, 17, 70
                        as relative clauses 16, 17, 70
    time clauses: "before" clauses 45
                     "until" clauses 25, 35, 37, 43, 45, 47, 51, 67
                     "when" clauses 36, 37
                     "while" clauses 46

Nouns
    appositives 67
    compound 15, 31, 47, 67, 68–69, 70, 79
    count and noncount 12, 38, 57, 61
    in a series 68, 80

Phrases
    infinitive phrases 23, 25, 65, 80, 84
    -ing phrases 18, 21, 23, 25, 42, 46, 84
    prepositional and adverb (locative) phrases:
        locative phrases 12, 15, 16, 21, 25, 29, 33, 35, 37, 38, 41, 42, 43, 44, 47, 56, 59, 65, 75, 77, 79, 84
        manner phrases 77
        "of" phrases: possessive 37, 61
                             possessive vs. genitive 75

Pronouns
    "one" 44, 49, 55
    possessive pronouns 46
    possessive pronouns used with parts of the body 33, 41, 42, 56

Questions
    indirect 17

Verbs
    compound verb 59
    contractions 43
    double-object verbs 70
    formation of negatives 13, 43
    "let" + bare infinitive 49
    "let" + noun phrase + bare infinitive 45
    passive voice 37, 51
    phrases joined by "or" or "and" 79
    that take particular prepositions 14, 31, 47, 57
    two-word verbs 16, 28, 31, 41, 49, 68, 70, 82, 84
    used as adjectives 19